SPOTLIGHT ON
IMMIGRATION AND MIGRATION

AFRICAN AMERICAN MIGRATIONS in NORTH AMERICA

Irene Harris

PowerKiDS
press™

NEW YORK

Published in 2016 by The Rosen Publishing Group, Inc.
29 East 21st Street, New York, NY 10010

Editor: Sarah Machajewski
Book Design: Samantha DeMartin

Photo Credits: Cover SuperStock/SuperStock/Getty Images; p. 4 Deeceevoice/Wikimedia Commons;
pp. 5, 7 Everett Historical/Shutterstock.com; pp. 9, 13, 14, 15, 17, 19 (Waller, Baker, Hughes), 21 Courtesy of
Library of Congress; p. 10 Courtesy of National Archives; p. 11 Library of Congress/Wikimedia Commons;
p. 19 (background) Herbert Gehr/The LIFE Picture Collection/Getty Images; p. 20 PhotoQuest/Archive Photos/
Getty Images; p. 22 Annie Leibovitz/Wikimedia Commons.

Cataloging-in-Publication Data

Harris, Irene.
African American migrations in North America / by Irene Harris.
p. cm. — (Spotlight on immigration and migration)
Includes index.
ISBN 978-1-5081-4046-7 (pbk.)
ISBN 978-1-5081-4047-4 (6 pack)
ISBN 978-1-5081-4049-8 (library binding)
1. African Americans — Migrations — History — Juvenile literature. 2. African Americans — History — Juvenile
literature. I. Harris, Irene. II. Title.
E185.H377 2016
973'.0496073—d23

Manufactured in the United States of America

CPSIA Compliance Information: Batch #BW16PK: For further information contact Rosen Publishing, New York, New York at 1-800-237-9932.

CONTENTS

FORCED TO LEAVE HOME

European explorers first arrived in North America in the late 15th century. In the years that followed, people from many nations came to live in the so-called New World. Many black Africans were first brought to America against their will. Taken from their native lands by force, the first Africans arrived in Jamestown, Virginia, in 1619.

The history of African people in America is one of severe hardship and immense **brutality**. During the 1600s, many slaves were sold to work on land that European **immigrants** were colonizing along North America's east coast. In America, the slave trade continued until the mid-1800s, when it was finally abolished, or legally ended. In the decades that followed, African Americans fought hard for their rightful and equal place in society.

Africans were transported across the Atlantic Ocean on huge slaving ships. This handbill advertises the sale of slaves that had just arrived in America from Sierra Leone.

5

SLAVERY IN THE UNITED STATES

Slavery was widespread throughout the American colonies, especially in the South. It continued well after the United States became an independent nation in 1783. Slaves were considered property and didn't have any **civil rights**. People began to question the morality of this, which means they questioned whether it was right or wrong to treat people as property.

In 1808, the U.S. government made the slave trade with Africa illegal, although it was still legal to buy and sell slaves already in the country. Southern **plantation** owners still depended on slave labor to grow tobacco, rice, and cotton. Between 1820 and 1860, southern plantation families owned 60 percent of the United States' slave population. By the early 1860s, there were about 4 million slaves in the southern states. Only a tiny percentage of blacks in the country lived outside the South.

Slaves were sold at public auctions. Families were torn apart when members were sold to people in different states or to faraway plantations. This included separating husbands from wives and parents from children.

ESCAPING SLAVERY

Many slaves were determined to be free, even if the law and society said they weren't. Many attempted to escape slavery by running away to the North, where blacks were free. This was extremely dangerous. Getting caught meant slaves were returned to their slave owners, or worse, killed.

Many slaves were aided by the Underground Railroad. It was a secret organization that helped thousands of slaves escape to freedom. Once they were free, the Underground Railroad helped former slaves find safe places to live.

Helping slaves run away was illegal. People in the Underground Railroad risked their lives to help slaves reach freedom. One such person was Harriet Tubman, a woman who escaped slavery in 1849. She then led hundreds of slaves to freedom, including her parents.

Harriet Tubman became an important figure in the antislavery movement. She often spoke out against slavery and was known for saying, "Live North, or die here."

FIGHTING FOR FREEDOM

The American Civil War began in 1861. One of the major causes of the war was the question of slavery. People in the North felt slavery should be illegal, while people in the South felt they needed it to keep their economy running. Eleven southern states **seceded** from the **Union** and formed the Confederate States of America, where they could practice slavery freely.

In 1863, President Abraham Lincoln issued the Emancipation Proclamation, which granted freedom to slaves in the states that had seceded. In January 1865, Congress passed the Thirteenth Amendment, officially abolishing slavery. The Union won the war in April of that year.

News of freedom spread throughout the South. By June, slaves had learned the news. When the Fourteenth Amendment passed in 1868, former slaves were now citizens of the United States.

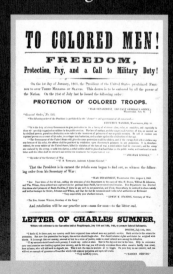

African American men were allowed to join the army after the Emancipation Proclamation was issued. About 179,000 black soldiers fought in the army and about 19,000 black soldiers fought in the navy, helping to secure a Union victory.

A NEW FORM OF SLAVERY

The Civil War destroyed the South. Its landscape and economy were in ruin. Life was very hard for former slaves. A group of white men formed the Ku Klux Klan in 1866. This group wore hoods and robes and existed to terrorize and kill blacks in the South.

Since many landowners refused to sell land to former slaves, blacks were forced to become sharecroppers. Sharecropping is a system in which a landowner allows **tenants** to use land in exchange for a portion of the crops grown on it. Landowners also rented tools and supplies at high interest rates. That means landowners charged a high fee in addition to what it cost to rent tools and supplies. This system became its own form of slavery. It kept many African Americans in **debt** and also kept them tied to the land. Many were forced to migrate in search of better opportunities.

This 1939 photograph shows a sharecropper who's been evicted, or forced out of his home and off his land. He's pictured carrying his belongings.

MIGRATING TO KANSAS

The **environment** in the South following the Civil War was so hostile that many African Americans were forced to leave. Between the late 1870s and 1890s, about 60,000 blacks migrated to Kansas. This migration was called the Great Exodus.

Benjamin "Pap" Singleton was one leader of this migration. He founded Dunlap Colony in Morris County, Kansas. By giving both advice and money, he helped thousands of blacks migrate to black colonies in Kansas. Many blacks were encouraged by his posters, which promised land, money, and freedom.

Ho for Kansas!

Brethren, Friends, & Fellow Citizens:
I feel thankful to inform you that the
REAL ESTATE
AND
Homestead Association,
Will Leave Here the
15th of April, 1878,
In pursuit of Homes in the Southwestern Lands of America, at Transportation Rates, cheaper than ever was known before.
For full information inquire of
Benj. Singleton, better known as old Pap,
NO. 5 NORTH FRONT STREET.
Beware of Speculators and Adventurers, as it is a dangerous thing to fall in their hands.
Nashville, Tenn., March 18, 1878.

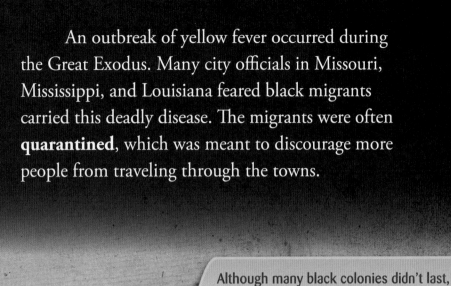

An outbreak of yellow fever occurred during the Great Exodus. Many city officials in Missouri, Mississippi, and Louisiana feared black migrants carried this deadly disease. The migrants were often **quarantined**, which was meant to discourage more people from traveling through the towns.

Although many black colonies didn't last, most blacks who left the South for them were glad they had. They finally knew what it felt like to own land as free people.

ECONOMIC OPPORTUNITIES

The 1900s through the 1960s saw another mass migration of African Americans. During this time, about 6 million blacks migrated from the South to the industrial North. This is known as the Great Migration.

The Great Migration occurred in waves that were directly related to the American economy. The first wave began in 1914 with World War I. There were fewer men to work in factories in cities such as Chicago, New York, Detroit, and St. Louis because fewer Europeans were coming to the United States. However, the factories still needed workers to make war-related products. Between 500,000 and 1 million African Americans migrated to cities to take these jobs.

The Great Depression in the 1930s, which was a time of economic suffering around the world, slowed migration. The start of World War II in 1939 strengthened the economy and encouraged migration again.

Factories in the North hired both black and white workers. The young boys and men in this picture worked in a glass factory.

A RENAISSANCE IN HARLEM

Harlem is a neighborhood in New York City. It was meant to be a white, upper-middle-class neighborhood. When the real estate market crashed in the early 20th century, whites didn't move in as planned. Educated, successful blacks did instead.

African Americans living in Harlem sent letters to southern relatives about their neighborhood. They wrote of the plentiful job opportunities there. This sparked a mass migration of blacks from the South beginning in 1910. By 1930, Harlem was the largest black neighborhood in the country. It had over 200,000 black residents. Many of them were accomplished writers, artists, and musicians. Notable residents, such as the writer Langston Hughes and the performer Josephine Baker, put Harlem on the map. The neighborhood became a place where black artists could freely explore and succeed in these talents.

The Harlem Renaissance of the 1920s was a movement that encouraged the creation of literature, art, and music that challenged racial **stereotypes**. It brought attention to important political and social problems, and encouraged African Americans to be proud of their race.

LANGSTON HUGHES (WRITER)

JOSEPHINE BAKER (PERFORMER)

FATS WALLER (MUSICIAN)

LIFE IN CHICAGO

Chicago, Illinois, is another important city in the history of African American migration. In 1905, a man named Robert S. Abbott began publishing the *Chicago Defender*. This newspaper encouraged blacks to move to Chicago and free themselves of oppression in the South. In 1890, Chicago's black population was about 15,000. By 1910, that number had increased to 40,000.

African Americans arrived in Chicago by train with no money, no jobs, and nowhere to live. The neighborhood where many blacks settled was called the Black Belt. The poorest blacks lived in the northern section of the belt. Wealthier blacks lived in the southern part. Jazz and blues, which were two popular styles of music, flourished in the southern neighborhoods.

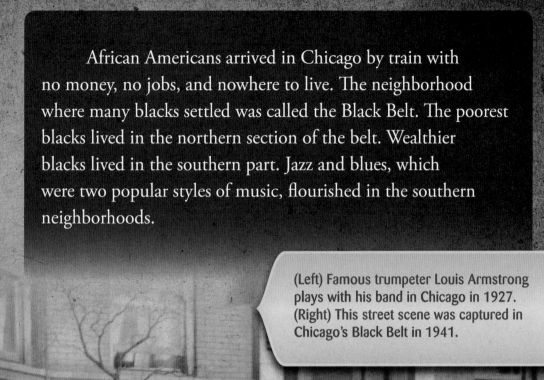

(Left) Famous trumpeter Louis Armstrong plays with his band in Chicago in 1927. (Right) This street scene was captured in Chicago's Black Belt in 1941.

FIGHTING FOR EQUALITY

Migration changed the way blacks in America lived. However, the changes weren't always easy. During the Great Migration in the early 20th century, tension between blacks and whites often resulted in violence. Racism was a normal practice, and schools and restaurants were **segregated**.

Laws and social customs made black people second-class citizens. They had to sit at the backs of buses and use separate restrooms. As blacks became more independent, they demanded equality and civil rights. They succeeded with the passage of the Civil Rights Act in 1964—100 years after slavery was abolished. African Americans had a grim start in America. Today, African Americans are leaders in all levels of society, including business, science, art, and more. Their spirit, strength, and determination are inspired by the hard fight for equality.

FIRST AFRICAN AMERICAN PRESIDENT AND FAMILY

GLOSSARY

brutality: Extreme physical violence.

civil rights: The rights of citizens to political and social freedom and equality.

debt: The state of owing money.

environment: The surroundings in which a person lives.

immigrant: A person who comes to live permanently in a new country.

plantation: Large farms on which cotton, tobacco, or sugarcane are grown.

quarantine: To separate a person who has been exposed to a contagious disease for a certain period of time.

secede: To formally withdraw from membership in a group.

segregate: To cause or force the separation of a group of people from the rest of society.

stereotype: A widely held view of a person, group, or subject that's based on general ideas formed without solid knowledge.

tenant: A person who occupies land or property rented from a landlord.

Union: The Northern, unified states of the United States that opposed the seceding of the Southern states during Civil War. Also, another name for the United States.

INDEX

PRIMARY SOURCE LIST

Page 4 (inset). Reproduction of a handbill advertising a slave auction in Charleston, South Carolina. Original, creator unknown, print on paper, July 24, 1769.

Page 10. Civil War recruitment poster. Written by the U.S. War Department. Ink on paper. 1863. Now kept at the Records of the Adjutant General's Office at the National Archives, College Park, MD.

Page 11. District of Columbia. Company E, 4th U.S. Colored Infantry, at Fort Lincoln. Created by William Morris Smith. Photograph. ca. 1863–1866. Now kept at the Library of Congress Prints and Photographs Division, Washington, D.C.

Page 14. "Ho For Kansas!" Copy print of handbill created by Benjamin Singleton. Ink on paper. Original created in 1878. Now kept at the Library of Congress Prints and Photographs Division, Washington, D.C.

WEBSITES

Due to the changing nature of Internet links, PowerKids Press has developed an online list of websites related to the subject of this book. This site is updated regularly. Please use this link to access the list: www.powerkidslinks.com/soim/afam